20 FUN FACTS ABOUT HALLOWEEN

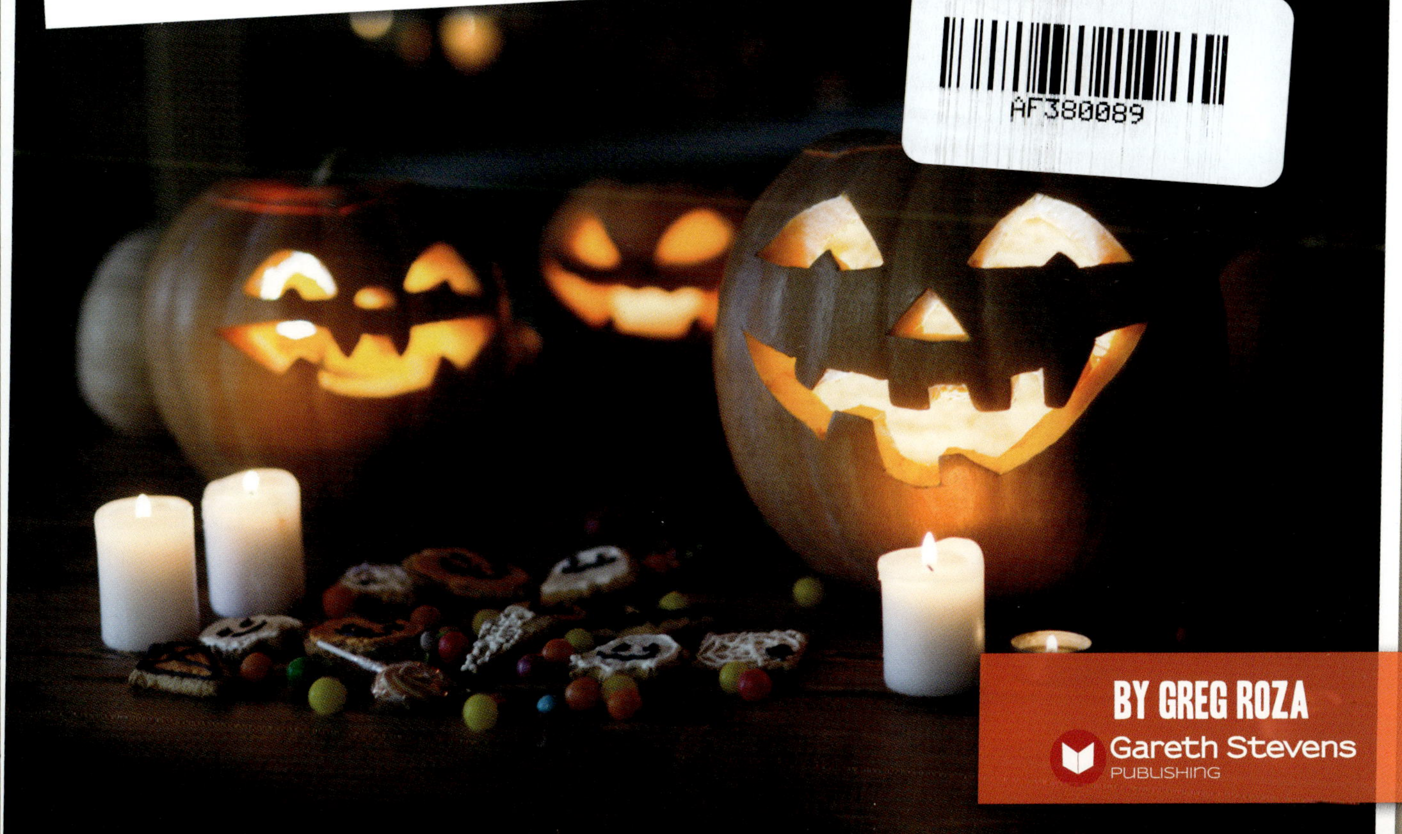

BY GREG ROZA

Gareth Stevens
PUBLISHING

Please visit our website, www.garethstevens.com. For a free color catalog of all our high-quality books, call toll free 1-800-542-2595 or fax 1-877-542-2596.

Library of Congress Cataloging-in-Publication Data
Names: Roza, Greg, author.
Title: 20 fun facts about Halloween / Greg Roza.
Other titles: Twenty fun facts about Halloween
Description: Buffalo, New York : Gareth Stevens Publishing, 2025 | Series:
    Fun fact file. The history of holidays | Includes index. | Audience:
    Grades 2-3
Identifiers: LCCN 2024000188 (print) | LCCN 2024000189 (ebook) | ISBN
    9781482466164 (library binding) | ISBN 9781482466157 (paperback) | ISBN
    9781482466171 (ebook)
Subjects: LCSH: Halloween–Juvenile literature.
Classification: LCC GT4965 .R69 2025 (print) | LCC GT4965 (ebook) | DDC
    394.2646–dc23/eng/20240108
LC record available at https://lccn.loc.gov/2024000188
LC ebook record available at https://lccn.loc.gov/2024000189

First Edition

Published in 2025 by
Gareth Stevens Publishing
2544 Clinton St
Buffalo, NY 14224

Copyright © 2025 Gareth Stevens Publishing

Editor: Therese Shea

Photo credits: Cover, p. 1 (main) Tiplyashina Evgeniya/Shutterstock.com; file folder used throughout David Smart/Shutterstock.com; binder clip used throughout luckyraccoon/Shutterstock.com; wood grain background used throughout ARENA Creative/Shutterstock.com; p. 5 Evgeny Atamanenko/Shutterstock.com; p. 6 Sunday Walk - British Museum (27147730088).jpg/Wikimedia Commons; p. 7 Nataliia Sokolovskaia/Shutterstock.com; p. 8 andreiuc88/Shutterstock.com; p. 9 Traditional Irish halloween Jack-o'-lantern.jpg/Wikimedia Commons; p. 10 A_Kool/Shutterstock.com; p. 11 Matt Benzero/Shutterstock.com; p. 12 James Kirkikis/Shutterstock.com; p. 13 Michael Warwick/Shutterstock.com; p. 14 Fountain of the Goddess Pomona 05.jpg/Wikimedia Commons; p. 15 Stefan Holm/Shutterstock.com; p. 16 Eve Orea/Shutterstock.com; p. 17 GEORGID/Shutterstock.com; p. 18 Emily van Wakeren/Shutterstock.com; p. 19 Photo Spirit/Shutterstock.com; p. 20 Trick or Treating - Beaumont, California (1950).png/Wikimedia Commons; p. 21 Snap-Apple Night globalphilosophy.PNG/Wikimedia Commons; p. 22 PeopleImages.com - Yuri A/Shutterstock.com; p. 23 Rawpixel.com/Shutterstock.com; p. 24 (main) Provincial Archives of Alberta/flickr; p. 24 (inset) Irish Halloween Mask at the Horniman Museum.jpg/Wikimedia Commons; p. 25 Kosoff/Shutterstock.com; p. 26 Trump White House Archives/flickr; p. 29 Tijana Moraca/Shutterstock.com.

Printed in the United States of America

Some of the images in this book illustrate individuals who are models. The depictions do not imply actual situations or events.

CPSIA compliance information: Batch #CS25GS: For further information contact Gareth Stevens, New York, New York at 1-800-542-2595.

CONTENTS

Words in the glossary appear in **bold** type the first time they are used in the text.

SPOOKY FUN!

Halloween is one of the most exciting holidays of the year for many people. Black cats, spooky bats, and grinning witches are some of the **symbols** of the holiday. Dressing up as scary monsters and trick-or-treating are popular parts of Halloween. And don't forget about making jack-o'-lanterns!

These aren't new **traditions**—at all! They're based on old, even ancient beliefs and traditions. Let's learn more about Halloween and all the spooky fun that comes with it!

A jack-o'-lantern is a pumpkin with its insides removed. It's then cut to look like a face or other shape.

ANCIENT TRADITIONS

THE ORIGINAL HALLOWEEN TOOK PLACE MORE THAN 2,000 YEARS AGO.

Halloween's start can be traced back to the ancient Celts. More than 2,000 years ago, these people **celebrated** Samhain (SOW-win) on October 31. They believed the living could talk to or even see the dead on this night.

The Celts were peoples of Central Europe. They later settled other areas, including what's now Ireland, Britain, France, and Spain. The Celts left behind art, like that shown here, that tells us about their traditional beliefs.

SAMHAIN HAD MANY OF THE SAME TRADITIONS AND SYMBOLS OF MODERN HALLOWEEN, SUCH AS MASKS, FIRES, FOOD, AND STORIES.

During Samhain celebrations, the Celts wore **costumes** of animal skins and told each other's **fortunes**. They burned crops and **sacrificed** animals to honor their gods.

FUN FACT: 3

THE WORD JACK-O'-LANTERN MAY COME FROM AN IRISH TALE.

In the story, a man named Jack cheats the **devil**. The devil gives Jack a piece of coal to light his way as he forever walks the earth. Jack became known as Jack of the **Lantern**—or later, jack-o'-lantern.

In the tale, Jack, or Stingy Jack, wasn't allowed to enter heaven or hell after he died. He had to walk the earth forever.

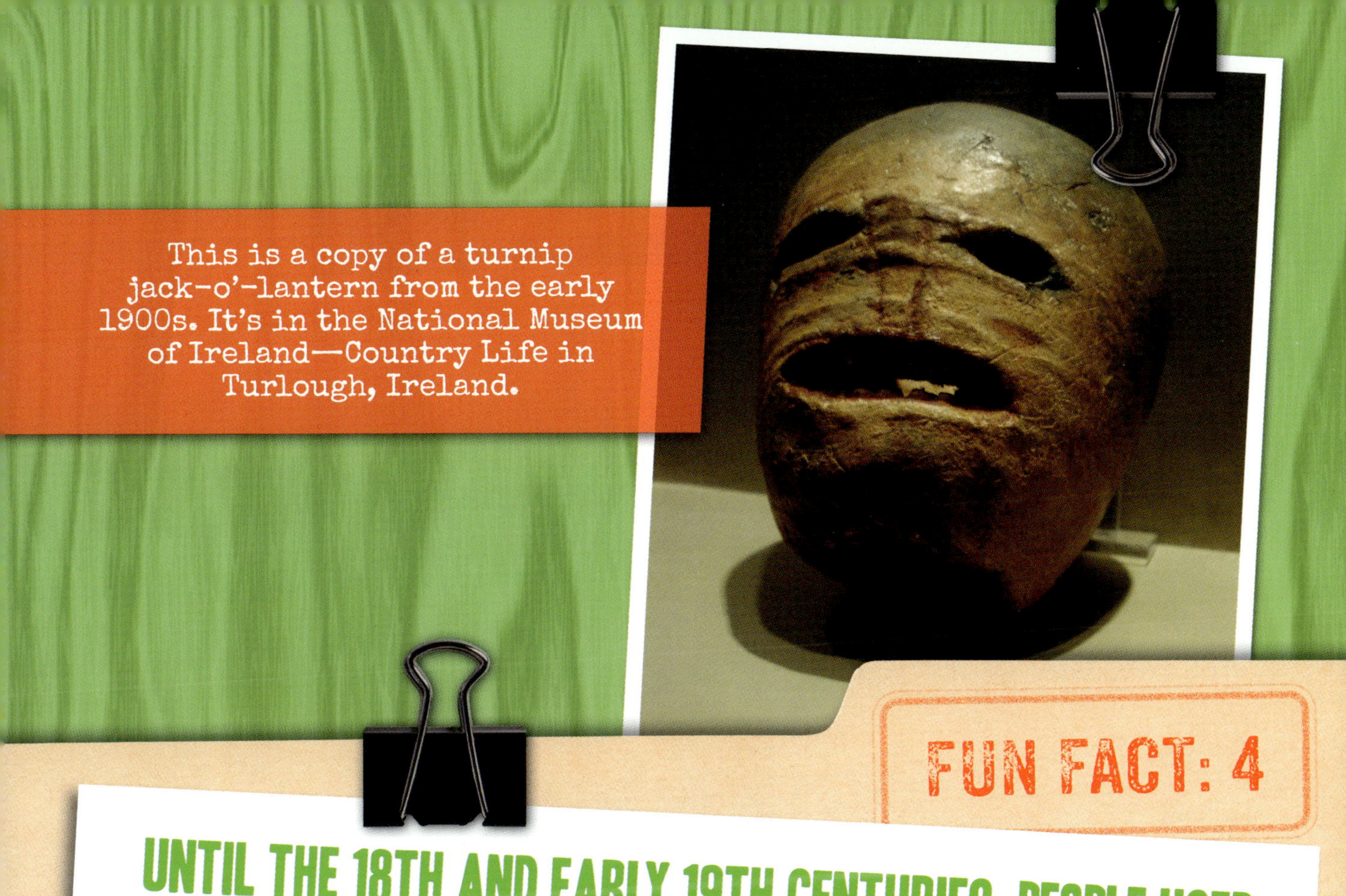

UNTIL THE 18TH AND EARLY 19TH CENTURIES, PEOPLE USED TURNIPS TO MAKE JACK-O'-LANTERNS.

In the jack-o'-lantern story, Jack cut into a turnip to hold his burning coal. In time, people in Ireland, England, and Scotland carved faces into turnips. They used them to scare off evil spirits.

KIDS HAVE LONG USED JACK-O'-LANTERNS TO TRICK AND SCARE OTHERS.

In a letter written in 1640, author James Howell wrote that "a Turnip cut like a Death's-head with a Candle in't [in it]" was used to scare "Boys and Women."

Jack-o'-lanterns have spooked people for centuries. Some today are funny-looking too!

THE JACK-O'-LANTERN TRADITION SWITCHED FROM CARVING TURNIPS TO CARVING PUMPKINS IN NORTH AMERICA.

Irish people brought Halloween traditions with them when they moved to North America in the 1800s. They found plentiful pumpkins. They discovered that pumpkins were easier to carve than turnips.

FUN FACT: 7

THE WORLD RECORD FOR THE MOST LIT JACK-O'-LANTERNS IN ONE PLACE AT ONE TIME IS 30,581!

This record was set in the city of Keene, New Hampshire, on October 19, 2013. Keene has been holding a pumpkin celebration since 1991.

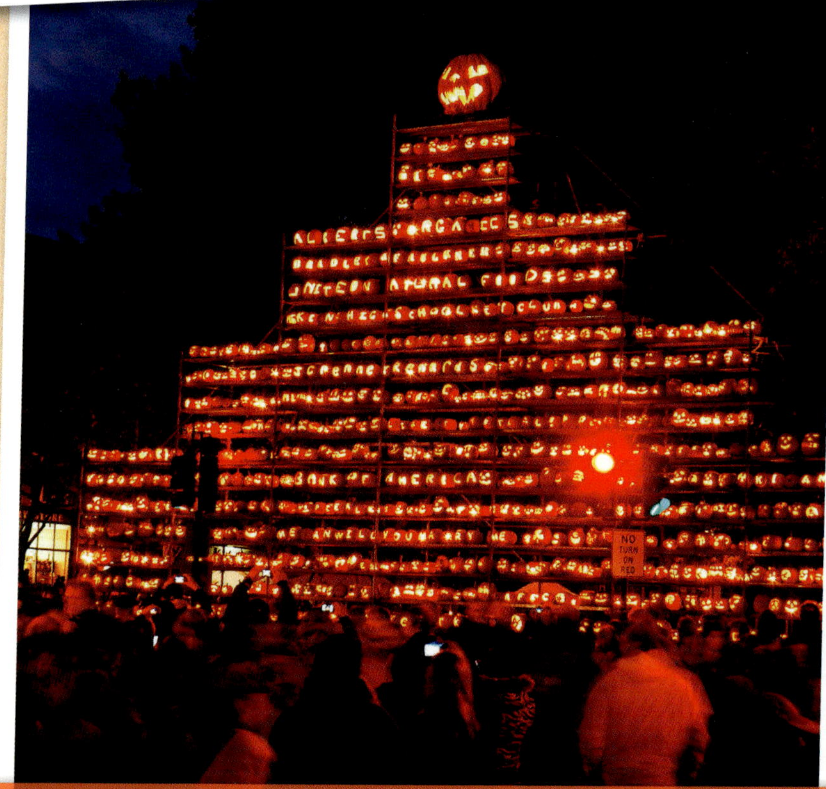

Keene's pumpkin celebration has broken the world record for the most lit jack-o'-lanterns eight times!

THE HEAVIEST JACK-O'-LANTERN WAS CARVED FROM A PUMPKIN THAT WEIGHED AS MUCH AS A SMALL CAR!

In 2023, a Minnesota teacher named Travis Gienger grew the heaviest pumpkin on record. It weighed 2,749 pounds (1246.9 kg). He named the pumpkin "Michael Jordan"!

CULTURAL INFLUENCES

THE ANCIENT ROMANS HELPED SHAPE TODAY'S HALLOWEEN.

The Romans had taken over most Celtic territory by the year 43. Samhain joined together with two Roman holidays. Feralia was a day when Romans honored the dead. Pomona honored the Roman goddess of fruit trees.

In artwork, the Roman goddess Pomona is often shown with apples.

THE WORD "HALLOWEEN" COMES FROM CHRISTIANITY.

In the year 837, the leader of the Catholic Church named November 1 All Saints' Day, or All Hallows' Day. ("Hallow" means "holy.") The night before became All Hallows' Eve, which became "Halloween."

15

MANY CULTURES HAVE CELEBRATIONS CENTERING ON THE DEAD.

One celebration is Día de los Muertos, or the Day of the Dead. It's based on a month-long celebration of the Native peoples of Mexico, but is now celebrated on November 1 and 2 in Latin American countries and the United States.

MORE WORLDWIDE SPIRITUAL CELEBRATIONS AND RITUALS

ALL SOULS' DAY

All Souls' Day, celebrated on November 2, is a day on which Christians pray for the dead who have not yet entered heaven.

OBON

Obon is a **Buddhist** festival in Japan in late summer, during which some believe the souls of the dead visit the living. Lanterns and fires are lit to guide the souls.

PANGANGALULUWA ("SOULING")

On All Saints' Day in the Philippines, groups of people visit houses to sing. The people represent, or stand for, souls asking for prayers from the living to help them get to heaven.

HUNGRY GHOST FESTIVAL

In Hong Kong, people celebrate the Hungry Ghost Festival sometime between mid-August and mid-September. People "feed" restless spirits, often by burning food and paper objects.

KUKERI FESTIVAL

In mid-winter, Bulgarian men dress as kukeri (KOO-kuh-ree), wearing monster costumes to drive away evil spirits. They parade through towns in their costumes and play music.

Kukeri costumes often include metal bells tied about the waist. The scary costumes and loud bells are meant to scare away evil spirits. Every community has its own kind of costume.

FUN FACT: 12

SOME BELIEVED WITCHES TURNED THEMSELVES INTO BLACK CATS.

That's one reason why black cats and witches are linked in tales. Some people thought black cats were witches' familiars too. Familiars are spirits that help witches do their magic.

Black cats are considered to be a lucky symbol in some places, such as Japan.

BATS HAVE BEEN A PART OF HALLOWEEN-LIKE CELEBRATIONS SINCE ANCIENT TIMES.

Samhain bonfires attracted bugs, which then drew bats because they eat bugs. The sight of bats at Samhain celebrations led to the belief that they're a sign of death.

FUN FACT: 14

HANDING OUT CANDY ON HALLOWEEN IS SOMEWHAT NEW.

Early Halloween traditions included asking for food from neighbors and celebrating with feasts. When trick-or-treating became popular in the United States, people handed out fruit, nuts, and coins. Today, candy is king!

Handing out candy became popular in the 1950s. Candy companies started producing smaller candy bars to hand out to kids for the holiday.

THE TRADITION OF BOBBING FOR APPLES IS LINKED TO ANCIENT FORTUNE-TELLING.

During the celebration of Pomona, Romans played games with apples to try to see into their futures. In more recent times, bobbing for apples was believed to be able to reveal, or show, if someone would marry soon.

FROM TRICKY MISCHIEF TO FAMILY FUN

FUN FACT: 16

THE TRADITION OF MAKING MISCHIEF WAS PART OF THE ORIGINAL SAMHAIN CELEBRATIONS.

Over the years, some young people have celebrated a "Mischief Night" by pranking, or tricking, others around Halloween. For places that celebrate, Mischief Night is often October 30.

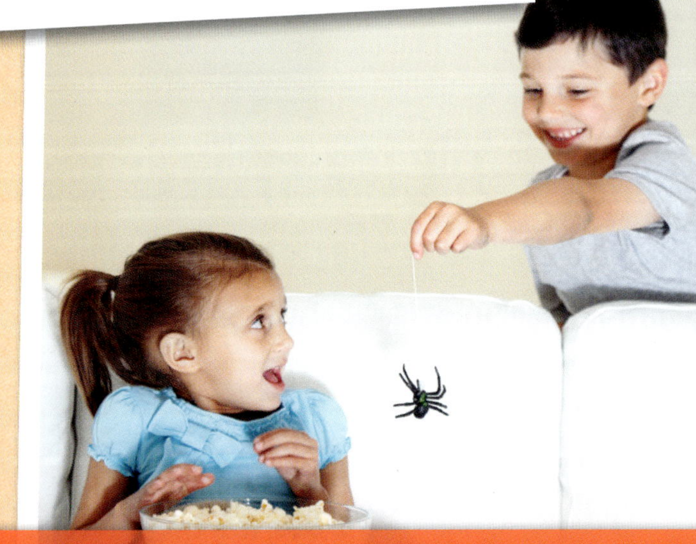

Mischief is any action that is meant to annoy but is not meant to cause real harm. Some mischief can turn out to be costly and dangerous though.

STARTING AROUND THE 1930s, HALLOWEEN BECAME MORE KID-FRIENDLY AND LESS MISCHIEVOUS.

For teens back then, pranking was a part of Halloween. But some threw stones, broke streetlights, and started fires. Some pranks resulted in deaths. Communities began to take action against mischief makers.

23

WORLD WAR II (1939-1945) INTERRUPTED AMERICAN HALLOWEEN PLANS.

During World War II, supplies needed for Halloween fun, including sugar, were low. Some cities cancelled activities. Cities also tried to crack down on mischief-causing kids during this time. They told them to support war efforts instead.

FUN FACT: 19

AMERICANS SPENT $10.6 BILLION ON HALLOWEEN IN 2022.

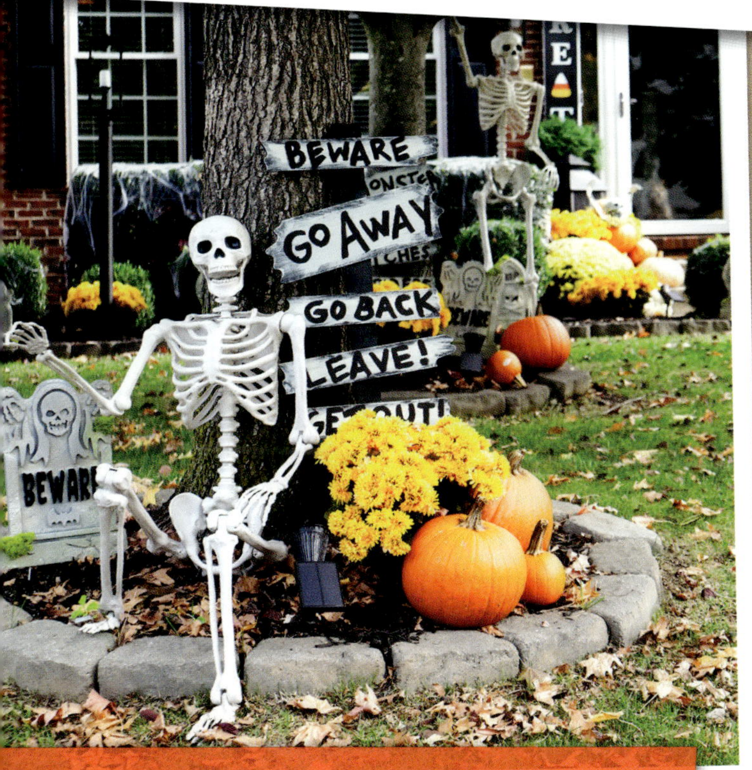

Some people decorate the inside and outside of their houses for Halloween.

Think of all the supplies needed for a successful Halloween party. They include spooky decorations, colorful costumes, yummy food, and of course, candy. Some people even buy costumes for their pets!

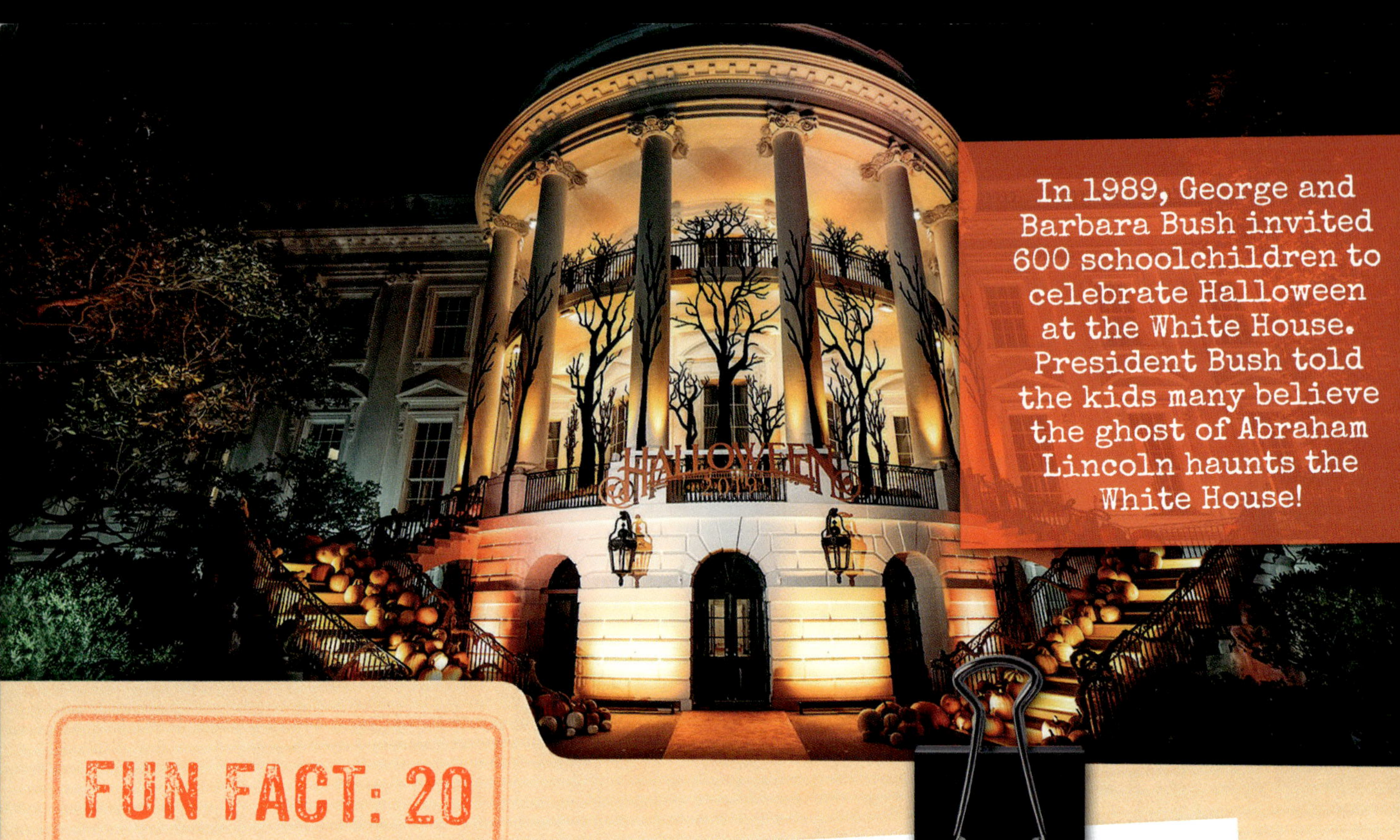

FUN FACT: 20

THE WHITE HOUSE HAS BEEN CELEBRATING HALLOWEEN SINCE 1958.

That year, First Lady Mamie Eisenhower decorated the White House for Halloween. Other presidents and first ladies continued the tradition. President John F. Kennedy was the first to invite children to the White House to trick-or-treat.

WHO HAUNTS THE WHITE HOUSE?

DAVID BURNES (1739-1799)
SOLD THE LAND ON WHICH MUCH OF WASHINGTON, DC, WAS BUILT

ABIGAIL ADAMS (1744-1818)
WIFE OF PRESIDENT JOHN ADAMS AND MOTHER TO PRESIDENT JOHN QUINCY ADAMS

ANDREW JACKSON (1767-1845)
SEVENTH PRESIDENT OF THE UNITED STATES

ABRAHAM LINCOLN (1809-1865)
SIXTEENTH PRESIDENT OF THE UNITED STATES

HARRY TRUMAN (1884-1972)
THIRTY-THIRD PRESIDENT OF THE UNITED STATES

THE "THING"
IN 1911, PRESIDENT WILLIAM HOWARD TAFT'S STAFF CLAIMED TO HAVE SEEN A TEENAGE BOY WHO LOOKED OVER PEOPLE'S SHOULDERS CALLED THE "THING."

The White House is the location of many ghost stories. Here are a few of the ghosts people have claimed to have seen.

BOO!

Today, kids love to wear scary or silly costumes and go trick-or-treating. Halloween parties may include bobbing for apples, but you're more likely to listen to ghost stories or go through a haunted house. Many adults also love to dress up in costumes for work and accompany their children while trick-or-treating. Some adults, as well as some kids, love to watch scary movies and holiday specials.

What's your favorite part of this spooky holiday? What traditions do you like to follow on Halloween?

Your Halloween traditions and the traditions of your community are a part of Halloween history too!

Buddhist: Having to do with a religion of eastern and central Asia based on the ancient teachings of the Buddha.

celebrate: To show happiness for an event through activities such as eating or playing music.

Christianity: A religion whose followers believe in the teachings of Jesus Christ.

costume: The clothes or other items worn by someone trying to look like someone or something else.

culture: The beliefs and ways of life of a group of people.

devil: A powerful spirit of evil in some religions.

fortune: What is to happen in the future.

lantern: A container with a handle for carrying a light source, such as a candle.

sacrifice: An offering to a god.

symbol: Something that stands for something else.

tradition: A way of life or an action that a group of people has practiced for a long time.

BOOKS

Salazar, Alicia. *Día de los Muertos.* North Mankato, MN: Pebble, 2022.

Spanier, Kristine. *Halloween.* Minneapolis, MN: Jump!, 2023.

Williams, Haley. *Halloween.* North Mankato, MN: ABDO, 2023.

WEBSITES

Playing It Safe on Halloween

kidshealth.org/en/kids/halloween-safety.html
Find out how to have fun and be safe while trick-or-treating.

Printable Jack O'Lantern Templates

www.personalcreations.com/blog/jack-o-lantern-templates
This website offers advice on how to prepare and care for your jack-o'-lantern and features printable jack-o'-lantern patterns.

White House Ghost Stories

www.whitehousehistory.org/press-room/press-backgrounders/white-house-ghost-stories
Read more spooky tales about the White House—if you dare!

INDEX